GALE
CENGAGE Learning

M000074353

Poetry for Students, Volume 59

Project Editor: Kristen A. Dorsch Rights Acquisition and Management: Ashley Maynard, Carissa Poweleit Composition: Evi Abou-El-Seoud Manufacturing: Rita Wimberley Imaging: John Watkins

Gale
27500 Drake Rd.
Farmington Hills, MI, 48331-3535

ISBN-13: 978-1-4103-6563-7
ISSN 1094-7019

This title is also available as an e-book.
ISBN-13: 978-1-4103-9310-4
ISBN-10: 1-4103-9310-4
Contact your Gale, A Cengage Company sales representative for ordering information.

Printed in Mexico

1 2 3 4 5 6 7 22 21 20 19 18

From Citizen, VI [On the Train the Woman Standing]

Claudia Rankine 2014

Introduction

The 2014 collection *Citizen: An American Lyric*, by award-winning writer Claudia Rankine, is a thought-provoking, uniquely styled statement about race issues in the United States in the twenty-first century. The book gathers everything from short anecdotes about the thoughtless remarks of coworkers to samples of visual art to pieces addressing racial aggression and violence. A well-known prose poem found in section VI of this volume is sometimes referred to by its opening phrase, "On the train the woman standing." The poem depicts the subtlety of racism faced by African Americans every day in modern society, describing an empty seat on a train declined by a female passenger because she is afraid of the man sitting next to it. Rankine cleverly confronts the reader with the woman's passive racism by casting the poem completely in the second person, forcing the reader to imagine one's own reaction to the situation.

Rankine was born in Kingston, Jamaica, on January 1, 1963. When she was seven years old, her family moved from Jamaica to New York. They settled in the Bronx, and Rankine was enrolled in a Catholic elementary school. She continued in parochial schools until her high-school graduation. Rankine then matriculated at Williams College, where she studied under Louise Glü ck, a talented poet who later earned a Pulitzer Prize and was named the US poet laureate. After receiving a bachelor's degree in 1986, Rankine continued her studies at Columbia University, earning a master of fine arts degree.

Through the first two decades of her career as a poet, Rankine has published five collections. Her first, *Nothing in Nature Is Private* (1994), was awarded the Cleveland State Poetry Prize. *TheEnd of the Alphabet*, her second collection, was published in 1998. *Plot* followed in 2001, a long, narrative poem about pregnancy and childbirth. *Don't Let Me Be Lonely: An American Lyric*, published in 2004, combines essays, poetry, and visual imagery in an in-depth examination of death. Her most recent collection is *Citizen: An American Lyric* (2014), which includes "VI [On the train the woman standing]."

Citizen was received with much acclaim; it was a finalist for the National Book Award and won the National Book Critics Circle Award in Poetry, the

PEN Center USA Poetry Award, the Forward Prize for Poetry, the Rebekah Johnson Bobbitt National Prize for Poetry, and the NAACP Image Award for Poetry. Rankine has been honored with many fellowships, including from the Guggenheim Foundation, the Academy of American Poets, the National Endowment for the Arts, the Lannan Foundation, and the John D. and Catherine T. MacArthur Foundation, with a MacArthur "genius grant." In 2005, the Academy of American Poets awarded Rankine the academy fellowship for distinguished poetic achievement.

In addition to her own books, Rankine's work has been featured in many prestigious anthologies, and she has worked as an editor on many poetry collections. She is also a playwright. Her 2009 play *The Provenance of Beauty: A South Bronx Travelogue* was commissioned by the Foundry Theatre, and she cowrote 2010's *Existing Conditions* with fellow playwright Casey Llewellyn. She was elected as an Academy of American Poets chancellor in 2013 and has taught at several prominent colleges across the country, including the University of Houston, the University of Georgia, Case Western Reserve University, Barnard College, Pomona College, and the University of Southern California. As of 2017, Rankine was serving as Yale University's Frederick Iseman Professor of Poetry.

Poem Summary

The text used for this summary is from *Citizen: An American Lyric*, Graywolf Press, 2014, pp. 131–33. A version of the poem can be found on the following web page: https://www.poets.org/poetsorg/poem/citizen-vi-train-woman-standing.

"On the train the woman standing" is a prose poem, with stanzas that look like paragraphs. The text is in the second person, meaning the speaker refers to the reader or listener as *you*.

Stanzas 1–2

The poem's first sentence describes the setting: a crowded train, likely a subway. There would seem to be no vacant seats, because a woman is standing, and yet a seat is apparently available. The speaker wonders if the woman might be standing because she is disembarking from the train very soon but then concludes that she refuses to sit—preferring to stand even if her stop is a long way off—because the only empty seat is next to a man she is afraid to sit close to. Although the poem does not specify the race of any of the people mentioned, the man is likely African American, and the woman is afraid to sit beside him because of prejudice and stereotypes surrounding African American men. That vacant seat takes on a special significance because of the woman's refusal to sit. The speaker explains, in the poem, how "you" sense the woman's fear but move past it as if it were a physical obstacle.

Stanza 3

You sit in the empty seat, but the man next to you does not react in any way. He is not surprised by the situation on the train. For him, instances of racism like this are so common that they no longer require conscious thought, much less elicit surprise. With repetition, slights like this have become as natural as breathing.

Stanza 4

When another person leaves the train and the standing woman takes the newly empty seat, it is clear beyond doubt that she simply did not want to sit next to your seatmate. You look at him, to gauge his response, but he shows no reaction. He stares out the train window. The speaker describes the view out the window as being "like darkness." This could be only a physical description: night could be falling, or the lights inside the train might reflect off the glass and make it difficult to see anything outside. However, the seeming darkness could also be metaphorical, portraying either the man's veiled anger or the blankness he imposes on his own thoughts and expression to protect himself from racist treatment.

Media Adaptations

- The Academy of American Poets posted a video of Rankine reading section VI of *Citizen* online at YouTube (https://www.youtube.com/watch?v=yMKhBkid9y0).

- Rankine reads another excerpt from *Citizen* at the 2014 Split This Rock Poetry Festival in a video also available on YouTube (https://www.youtube.com/watch?v=Q3NwwP4w4wI).

- In a clip from *PBS News Hour*, Rankine explains some of what she was trying to accomplish with the poems in *Citizen* (https://www.youtube.com/watch?v=i-SNKU3T7iA).

- Focusing in particular on issues of race, Rankine discusses *Citizen* in an interview at the *Los Angeles Times* Festival of Books (https://www.youtube.com/watch?v=upCFbREUvtk).

Stanza 5

Stanza 5 lists many locations where one might be required to sit near strangers, and the speaker assigns you the willingness to remain with your seatmate in any one of these places. This willingness to physically align yourself with the man represents a sympathetic bond with his struggle and empathy for the unfair treatment he faces every day.

Stanzas 6–7

The speaker speculates about your thoughts as you ride the train, sitting next to the man. There is a feeling of urgency and discomfort, because you want to help, yet although you occupy the physical seat, there is no way to fill the blankness that surrounds the man—the metaphorical unoccupied train seat—because of his race and the way people react to it. When the man leaves the train, he will take that emptiness with him. He cannot leave it behind, and you cannot ameliorate it or erase it.

Stanzas 8–9

Stanzas 8 and 9 explore how the man might feel behind his inexpressive façade. The speaker posits that if he talked, he would claim that he was fine and relieve you of the necessity of sitting next to him. The train passes into a tunnel, and the lack of light inside it provides privacy for you to study the man, wondering if he realizes he is being watched. He likely knows, and the speaker questions the meaning of suspicion as well as its effects.

Stanzas 10–11

The fabric of your jacket touches the man's sleeve. Although your shoulders are aligned while seated in the train, if you were both on your feet he might be taller than you, casting you in shadow. You wonder what you hope to fix by sitting in the seat and also if it is past time for anything to be fixed. There might never be a good time to fix this problem. Just as the train moves too quickly for you to be able to discern the details of your surroundings, such as the lights and tiles on the wall of the tunnel outside the window, the world moves and changes too quickly for people to figure out the right time to solve society's problems.

Stanza 12

You overhear a woman asking another passenger if he would be willing to change his seat so that she can sit with her child. The language of the first sentence in this stanza pushes the reader to imagine a similar exchange happening anywhere in the world—not just elsewhere in the train but on the other side of a room or even a body of water. You are somehow cut off from this conversation, unable to hear or see properly.

Stanza 13

The man in the seat next to you turns. Although he still does not speak, you express a determination not to move from your seat, even if asked to do so. You will insist on staying together, as if you and the man, like the woman and her child a few rows in front of you, are members of the same family.

Themes

Racism

At the center of this poem, indeed, at the center of every selection in the collection, is the theme of racism. In *Citizen*, Rankine illustrates some of the countless examples of racism faced every day by African Americans. Sometimes the hatred and prejudice erupt into violence, but in this particular piece, the racism is subtle. It is displayed not by words or even actions, but instead by a lack of action: the woman on the train declining an unoccupied seat on a subway train evidently because she does not like the look of the man sitting next to it.

The observer—the "you" of the poem—sees the woman standing and tries to give her the benefit of the doubt, thinking she might remain standing only because the train is close to her stop. However, the woman does not get off the train soon, and when another seat becomes available, she takes it. Upon understanding this, you perceive how evidence of this kind of subtle racism has habituated the man to such treatment. He no longer has to think about it, because it has become as commonplace as breath, as if with every inhalation he is forced to also take in suspicion and latent hatred.

This exploration of racism is particularly interesting because it concerns a sort that is easily ignored. Race is pushed to the forefront of people's attention when they see photos of KKK rallies or video of an African American man being brutalized by white police officers. It is easy to distance oneself from such extreme cases, seen only online or on television news programs, whereas the situation described in the poem is one any person of color might face on any given day. Because the racism illustrated by the woman's refusal to sit on the train next to the African American man is so subtle—so seemingly unimportant and harmless—this kind of incident is often dismissed. However, the attitudes that contribute to such behavior are the same ones that lead to violence. The fact that this example shows a less dramatic, nonviolent result does not erase the serious problem at the heart of the issue.

Compassion

Rankine does not specify the race of any of the people in the poem, but it is logical to conclude that the man next to the vacant seat is African American. Because the standing woman sees the color of his skin, she makes certain judgments about him and decides to keep her distance. The observer in the poem, however, sees the situation and is filled with compassion for the man. Though he bears this unfair treatment without revealing any emotional reaction, the observer wants to sit with the man to show her support. Indeed, even after she settles into her seat, her thoughts and behavior are driven by the need to "keep trying to fill" the metaphorical empty seat created by the standing woman's racism.

The fact that Rankine does not indicate the race of the observer becomes an effective tool, because whether "you" are an African American who knows all too well how the man feels or a white passenger realizing for the first time how constant, subtle racism affects minority people in their day-to-day lives, what is important in the observer's reaction is the compassion felt. Rather than seeing the man and judging him based on his appearance, the observer sees his situation and imagines how he must feel. This compassion leads the observer to a deep empathy for the man, to the point of proclaiming, in the final lines of the poem, the desire to align as family. If everyone allowed themselves to feel this kind of compassion, the poem suggests, people would not be so quick to judge unfairly and be guided by knee-jerk reactions based on ignorant fear.

Prose Poetry

Rather than being written in rhyming lines or metered stanzas, this poem reads more like prose than poetry. The stanzas look like paragraphs. While it is not as traditional, this style is extremely approachable. Readers not comfortable with the formal structure of sonnets and the strict rhyme schemes of more traditional styles might be willing to give this a try, thereby expanding Rankine's audience and potentially spreading her important message more widely.

Topics for Further Study

- Read Angie Thomas's 2017 young-adult novel *The Hate U Give*, in which sixteenyear-old protagonist Starr sees her childhood friend Khalil shot and killed by a police officer. Starr already feels torn between the poverty-stricken neighborhood where she grew up and her elite private school in the suburbs, and the controversy surrounding Khalil's death highlights the conflict between the two halves of her life. Write an essay comparing how Thomas and Rankine tackle issues of race and prejudice.

- Sketch or paint a picture of the scene of the poem, taking particular care to depict the expressions on the faces of the train's passengers in a way that makes their reactions to the situation clear.

- Write a poem about a tense situation and a person showing support in a subtle way. Mimic the narrative style Rankine uses in section VI of *Citizen*.

- Create a website featuring poems that deal with issues of race, prejudice, and stereotyping. Invite classmates and friends to comment and contribute their own suggestions for literature dealing with these themes.

Critic Holly Bass of the *New York Times* explains that although "Rankine has for the most part abandoned line breaks," creating her distinguished prose-like style, that does not mean that her straightforward, relatively simple language should not be considered poetry. "She is like a painter abandoning representation in order to focus on canvas, color and light," Bass writes. The critic continues: "In her world, enjambment, that poetic technique of allowing a sentence to run into the next line of poetry, often to create layered meanings, takes place between poems rather than between lines."

The *New Yorker*'s Dan Chiasson points out another effect of Rankine's style in *Citizen*. He notes that "the rectilinear language blocks that make up much of *Citizen* suggest the prose poem, that hand-me-down from the French Symbolists." However, Chiasson highlights the effectiveness of the prose style in adding to the works' realism. He wonders if their matter-offact tone might be "non-literary," drawn from

> the police log, the journal entry, or—
> a new form familiar to anybody who
> visits student unions—the confession
> board papered with anonymous note
> cards. Rankine's prose
> representations often border on *pro
> se* representation, the action of
> defending oneself in a court of law.

With her simple language and her prose style, Rankine proves that poetry can rely on elements other than meter and rhyme to create meaning and mood.

Second-Person Narration

Perhaps Rankine's boldest choice in *Citizen* is having the speaker address readers as "you" rather than simply describing each scene in the first person, a far more common choice in poetry. By using the second-person voice, Rankine confronts readers and forces them to think about what their own reactions would be to the situations described. When readers see "you" on the page, they put themselves into the train with the racist standing woman and the blank-faced man sitting next to an empty seat. They ask themselves whether they would, as described in the poem, feel compassion for the man and move quickly past the woman and her fear to sit beside him, or whether they would be paralyzed by fear of a negative stereotype and cower by the door, pretending not to see the vacant seat.

The use of the second person allows Rankine to highlight issues of race in her work. Bass points out that when reading the poems in *Citizen*,

> it's easy to presume the "you" is always black and the "she" or "he" is always white, but within a few pages Rankine begins muddying the personas and pronouns in a way that

forces us to work a little harder.

In "On the train the woman standing," for example, "you" might be an African American, sitting with the man in solidarity. Or "you" might be white, identifying for the first time with someone who must often face such pernicious, if subtle, racism. By including the simple pronoun without any identifying characteristics, Rankine does not specify the race of the observer, or indeed of any of the various characters, which adds other levels of possible interpretation and forces the reader to think about his or her own preconceived ideas regarding the situation.

Racial Tensions Running High in America

At the time when Rankine was composing and publishing her collection *Citizen*, racial issues were prominent in American headlines. In February 2012, Trayvon Martin, a seventeen-year-old African American in Sanford, Florida, was shot and killed by neighborhood watchman George Zimmerman. Martin did not have a spotless record; at the time, he was on a ten-day suspension from school because drug residue had been discovered in his backpack. Zimmerman maintained throughout his trial that Martin attacked him, forcing him to draw his gun in self-defense. However, Zimmerman, when he called to report suspicious activity, had been specifically instructed by a 911 dispatcher not to approach the boy, and Martin was unarmed, carrying only his phone and the soda and candy he had purchased at a convenience store minutes before. The jury found Zimmerman not guilty, and in 2015, the Justice Department announced that no federal civil rights charges would be filed against him.

Adding to racial tension in the country were highly publicized cases where African American men were killed during arrests by white police officers using what proved to be excessive force. In July 2014, the arrest of Eric Garner, who had been selling loose cigarettes on a Staten Island street, was recorded on video. Officer Daniel Pantaleo held Garner in a chokehold, and the video captures Garner saying, "I can't breathe." Garner died, and protests erupted when Pantaleo was not charged. Tempers flared even more with the news that Pantaleo, now on modified duty, got a raise the following year and, as of 2017, still has not faced an official departmental review, despite an additional fourteen complaints being filed against him.

Only one month after Garner's death, Officer Darren Wilson fatally shot African American teenager Mike Brown in Ferguson, Missouri. Surveillance cameras at the Ferguson Market and Liquor caught video of a man believed to be Brown stealing a box of cigarillos and pushing a clerk on his way out of the store. Outside in the street a couple of blocks away, there was a tussle between Wilson and Brown before the latter took off running with his friend. However, eyewitness accounts of what happened next vary greatly. Some witnesses say that when Wilson fired the fatal shots, Brown was turning toward the officer, hands up as if intending to surrender. Others believe Brown intended to rush at the officer and attack him.

Black Lives Matter cofounder Alicia Garza cites deaths like these—specifically mentioning Martin and Brown by name—as the catalyst for the formation of the organization. Garza, working with Patrisse Cullors and Opal Tometi, started Black Lives Matter as "a call to action and a response to the virulent anti-Black racism that permeates our society" and a "unique contribution that goes beyond extrajudicial killings of Black people by police and vigilantes." The organization sees itself as

> an ideological and political intervention in a world where Black lives are systematically and intentionally targeted for demise. It is an affirmation of Black folks' humanity, our contributions to this society, and our resilience in the face of deadly oppression.

Garza, Cullors, and Tometi were determined to take their movement beyond the usual civil rights efforts, which tend to be led and motivated by men, while "our sisters, queer and trans and disabled folk take up roles in the background or not at all." Instead, Black Lives Matter works to uphold "the lives of Black queer and trans folks, disabled folks, undocumented folks, folks with records, women and all Black lives along the gender spectrum"—those who have traditionally "been marginalized within Black liberation movements." Some take offense at the name of the organization, as if it implies that *only* the lives of African Americans are important, but rather Black Lives Matter exists to draw attention to a basic inequality in American society,

> broadening the conversation around state violence to include all of the ways in which Black people are intentionally left powerless at the hands of the state. We are talking

about the ways in which Black lives
are deprived of our basic human
rights and dignity.

Compounding the problem are the vast
differences in how people perceive the situation.
Polling reported in 2014 by Lindsey Cook in *U.S.
News & World Report* shows the gulf between
Americans' opinions about such issues as justice,
the role of police in keeping people safe, and
whether the government should or can get involved
in such concerns. After the advances of the civil
rights movement, African Americans were more
optimistic than their white counterparts when it
came to race relations, believing that eventually the
conflict would be resolved. However, as the years
passed, that optimism lessened, until in the early
1990s, white and African American opinions were
approximately the same, with 44 percent of both
groups believing racial conflict in the United States
would eventually work out. Since then, other than a
brief surge in confidence after the election of
President Barack Obama, optimism in African
American communities regarding race relations has
lagged far behind that of white Americans.

The 2014 Cook article shows that many
African Americans believe that they have a much
lower chance of getting a job for which they are
qualified than a white American has. Also, the
statistics indicate that African Americans see
unfairness in many other aspects of society, such as
in the courtroom and while voting. Whereas 70
percent of African Americans stated that they feel

blacks are treated less fairly than whites when dealing with the police, only 37 percent of whites agreed. Only 17 percent of white Americans indicated in the poll that they feel new civil rights legislation is needed to fight discrimination, compared to 53 percent of African Americans.

The political climate remains charged, and the issues of race and equality often become tangled up with other controversial debates, such as freedom of speech, as can be seen in the media storm surrounding NFL players taking a knee during the national anthem. From a survey of the violent interactions emblematic of racial issues today along with the statistics of scientific polling, it is clear that America still has a long road ahead. Literary works like Rankine's that portray and explore these situations are vitally important in efforts to understand and resolve racial conflict.

Critical Overview

For *Citizen*, Rankine was nominated for numerous poetry awards and won several, including the National Book Critics Circle Award, the PEN/Open Book Award, the Los Angeles Times Book Prize, and the NAACP Image Award, among others. The collection was also a *New York Times* best seller, proving that Rankine's thoughtful, hard-hitting work is fascinating to readers, and critics were impressed. In fact, critics praised the book even when they did not quite know what to make of it. In addition to earning the National Book Critics Circle Award for Poetry, *Citizen* was also a finalist for that organization's award for Criticism. The London *Guardian*'s Kate Kellaway explains that although the

> book may or may not be poetry—the question becomes insignificant as one reads on. Her achievement is to have created a bold work that occupies its own space powerfully, an unsettled hybrid—her writing on the hard shoulder of prose.

Rankine's unique style intrigues readers and critics alike and subtly includes everyone in the examination of the problem of racism—perhaps implicating everyone as well. As Kellaway remarks in highlighting Rankine's use of a second-person narrative voice, "There is no first person here, just a 'you' to keep things free…. I am conscious of the friction between my wish to pin things down and Rankine's to pull towards universality."

Holly Bass of the *New York Times* agrees that Rankine does a remarkable job in "making racism relevant, or even evident, to those who do not bear the brunt of its ill effects," by "brilliantly push[ing] poetry's forms to disarm readers and circumvent our carefully constructed defense mechanisms against the hint of possibly being racist ourselves." Though Rankine's style in *Citizen* seems more prose than poetry, Bass praises how "the writing zigs and zags effortlessly between prose poems, images and essays. This is the poet as conceptual artist, in full mastery of her craft." According to Bass, Rankine masterfully "creates an intentionally disorienting experience, one that mirrors the experience of racial microaggressions her subjects encounter. Race is both referenced and purposely effaced within the text."

Critic Dan Chiasson, writing for the *New Yorker*, describes the collection as a "book-length poem about race and the imagination" and a "brilliant, disabusing work, always aware of its ironies." Chiasson marvels at how Rankine vividly portrays "the acts of everyday racism—remarks, glances, implied judgments—that flourish in an environment where more explicit acts of discrimination have been outlawed." In addition, Chiasson highlights Rankine's references to popular culture and current events, pointing out how "*Citizen* conducts its business, often, with melancholy, but also with wit and a sharable incredulity that sends you running to YouTube."

Daniel Worden, in introducing a symposium on *Citizen* for the *Los Angeles Review of Books*, comes to the fundamental point of the collection. It can be considering poetry or prose, literature or criticism, but its basic political nature cannot be ignored. As Worden writes, the book "must be read as both a poetic work and a political work, a meditation on activist struggles and literary aesthetics."

What Do I Read Next?

- In Rankine's second collection, *TheEnd of the Alphabet* (1998), she experiments with adopting familiar voices from literature, such as those of Lady Macbeth and Jane Eyre.

- *Mexican WhiteBoy* (2008), by Matt

de la Peña, tells the story of teenager Danny, son of a white European American mother and a Mexican father. Danny feels trapped by people's expectations based solely on how he looks. He travels to Mexico to be with his father for a while in the hope of better understanding where he came from and who he would like to become.

- The ties between location and race relations, as well as how the boundaries and differences between communities reflect racial prejudice and inequality, are analyzed in *Race and Place: Equity Issues in Urban America* (2003), by John W. Frazier, Florence M. Margai, and Eugene Tettey-Fio.

- In the anthology *Of Poetry and Protest: From Emmett Till to Trayvon Martin* (2016), editors Phil Cushway and Michael Warr have gathered the work of more than forty poets spanning the preceding half century on the subject of race and politics in the United States.

- Young-adult author Nic Stone's 2017 novel *Dear Martin* is named for the journal kept by the protagonist, Justyce McAllister, who addresses his entries to Dr. Martin

Luther King Jr., hoping to gain inspiration and wisdom from his example. Though he is a brilliant student and an all-around good kid, Justyce faces the prejudice of a white cop, who arrests him.

- The children of interracial marriages are often victims of racism from people who share only part of their heritage. Editor Pearl Fuyo Gaskins interviewed mixed-race teens and collected some of their most interesting insights in *What Are You? Voices of Mixed-Race Young People* (1999).

- The danger of stereotyping was shown in an extreme form in the Holocaust. Newbery medalist Jerry Spinelli's 2003 young-adult novel *Milkweed* portrays a Jewish orphan, living on the streets of Warsaw, who admires the smart uniforms and shiny boots of the Nazi officers until he understands that the people living in the Jewish ghetto are being taken away by trains, never to be seen again.

Sources

"About," Black Lives Matter website, http://blacklivesmatter.com/about/ (accessed October 2, 2017).

Bass, Holly, Review of *Citizen*, in *New York Times*, December 28, 2014, https://www.nytimes.com/2014/12/28/books/review/rankines-citizen.html?mcubz=1 (accessed October 2, 2017).

Chiasson, Dan, "Color Codes," in *New Yorker*, October 27, 2014, https://www.newyorker.com/magazine/2014/10/27/c codes (accessed October 2, 2017).

Clarke, Rachel, and Christopher Lett, "What Happened When Michael Brown Met Officer Darren Wilson," CNN website, November 11, 2014, http://www.cnn.com/interactive/2014/08/us/fergusor brown-timeline/ (accessed October 2, 2017).

"Claudia Rankine," Poetry Foundation website, https://www.poetryfoundation.org/poets/claudia-rankine (accessed September 21, 2017).

"Claudia Rankine," Poets.org, https://www.poets.org/poetsorg/poet/claudia-rankine (accessed September 21, 2017).

Cook, Lindsey, "Blacks and Whites See Race Issues Differently," in *U.S. News & World Report*, December 15, 2014, https://www.usnews.com/news/blogs/datamine/2014/12/15/blacks-and-whites-see-race-issues-differently (accessed October 2, 2017).

Fox, Alison, "Eric Garner's Death, and Where the Investigation, People Are Now," in *am New York*, July 17, 2017, http://www.amny.com/news/eric-garner-s-death-and-where-the-investigation-people-are-now-1.12048636 (accessed October 2, 2017).

"Herstory," Black Lives Matter website, http://blacklivesmatter.com/herstory/ (accessed October 2, 2017).

James, Sherman A., "John Henryism and the Health of African-Americans," in *Culture, Medicine and Psychiatry*, Vol. 18, no. 2, 1994, pp. 163–82, https://deepblue.lib.umich.edu/bitstream/handle/202? sequence=1 (accessed October 16, 2017).

Kellaway, Kate, "*Citizen: An American Lyric* by Claudia Rankine Review: The Ugly Truth of Racism," in *Guardian* (London, England), August 30, 2015, https://www.theguardian.com/books/2015/aug/30/cl? rankine-citizen-american-lyric-review (accessed October 2, 2017).

Rankine, Claudia, "On the train the woman standing," in *Citizen: An American Lyric*, Graywolf Press, 2014, pp. 131–33.

Serafin, Steven R., "Claudia Rankine," in *Encyclopædia Britannica*, August 3, 2017, https://www.britannica.com/biography/Claudia-Rankine (accessed September 21, 2017).

"Trayvon Martin Shooting Fast Facts," CNN

website, June 22, 2017, http://www.cnn.com/2013/06/05/us/trayvon-martin-shooting-fast-facts/index.html (accessed October 2, 2017).

Worden, Daniel, "On Claudia Rankine's *Citizen: An American Lyric*: A Symposium, Part I," in *Los Angeles Review of Books*, January 6, 2016, https://lareviewofbooks.org/article/reconsidering-claudia-rankines-citizen-an-american-lyric-a-symposium-part-i/#! (accessed October 2, 2017).

Further Reading

Hughes, Langston, *The Collected Poems of Langston Hughes*, edited by Arnold Rampersad, Vintage, 1995.

> Hughes was one of the most beloved writers of the Harlem Renaissance, and his poems tackled many contemporary issues, including racial tension and stereotypes. This collection gathers all of his over eight hundred published poems in chronological order.

Rankine, Claudia, *Nothing in Nature Is Private*, Cleveland Poetry Center, 1995.

> This edition of Rankine's first collection was released by the Cleveland Poetry Center, which gave the book an award.

Rankine, Claudia, Beth Loffreda, and Max King Cap, eds., *The Racial Imaginary: Writers on Race in the Life of the Mind*, Fence Books, 2015.

> In 2011, Rankine wrote an open letter responding to the work of a white male poet, particularly a poem that referenced a black woman's body. In this collection, poets from varied backgrounds address the issue of how societal conditions affect the

creation of their work.

Reynolds, Jason, and Brendan Kiely, *All American Boys*, Atheneum/Caitlyn Dlouhy Books, 2015.

> Reynolds and Kiely wrote this novel in tandem, alternating chapters between two teenaged boys: Rashad and Quinn. When Quinn's adoptive father, Paul, a police officer, suspects Rashad of shoplifting and then resisting arrest, tensions in the community erupt. Some are certain Paul used excessive force because Rashad is African American. Quinn, however, does not want to believe it.

Steele, Claude M., *Whistling Vivaldi: And Other Clues to How Stereotypes Affect Us*, W. W. Norton, 2010.

> Through fascinating anecdotes and analysis, Steele illustrates the damaging effects of stereotypes. In one experiment, math majors are told just before a test that women are often thought to have weaker math skills than men—and the female students do not do as well as expected. Steele shows how internalizing negative stereotypes can undermine individual identity and suggests some ways to reduce the negative impact.

Suggested Search Terms

Claudia Rankine

Claudia Rankine AND "On the train the woman standing"

Claudia Rankine AND Citizen AND review

Claudia Rankine AND race issues

Claudia Rankine AND Citizen AND review

racial profiling AND America

prose poetry

Black Lives Matter

poetry AND politics